AF407819

My Books:

"How to Live with Bipolar"

"Bipolar 1 Disorder Rescue Plan"

"37 Symptoms of Bipolar Depression" (workbook)

"The Bipolar Disorder Guide"

"A Practical Guide to Overcoming Loneliness"

"We Never Did Mornings" (poetry)

THE BIPOLAR DISORDER GUIDE

Overcome challenges & find your path to wellness

Famous People With Bipolar Disorder

Kanye West
Mariah Carey
Carrie Fisher
Mel Gibson
Demi Lovato
Maria Bamford
Catherine Zeta-Jones
Frank Sinatra
David LaChapelle
Sinead O'Connor
Jean-Claude Van Damme
Jane Pauley
Patty Duke
Linda Hamilton
Mariette Hartley
Selena Gomez
Scott Stapp
Maurice Bernard
David Harbour
Amy Winehouse
Halsey
Richard Dreyfuss
Russell Brand
Kurt Cobain
Grahame Greene
Nina Simone
Sir Winston Churchill
Vincent Van Gogh
Virginia Wolf
Ernest Hemingway
Buzz Aldrin
Florence Nightingale
Sting
Isaac Newton
William Blake
Beethoven
Theodore Roosevelt

Contents

Introduction

You are not feeling well, you go to see a psychiatrist, he or she gives you a diagnosis of bipolar disorder and you walk out clutching a prescription in your hand.

How common is that? More common than you might think.

Doctors are busy people. They don't make the time to educate people when they give out a diagnosis. They expect you to do the research yourself. You look down at the prescription in your hand and wonder what to do next.

Hold on! Don't get overwhelmed. Go home and read this little book instead.

This is a book about all the basics you need to know to get well and stay well with bipolar disorder. There is no doubt about it, the diagnosis is overwhelming at first. You might even think the psychiatrist has got it all wrong. Surely, you don't have bipolar disorder! You don't have a mental illness. Your doctor must have made a mistake.

However, if you have been ill for some time, you might be relieved to know you have bipolar disorder. That is good. But you will still need to read this book.

You would never believe how many people deny the diagnosis of bipolar disorder. It is certainly not something nice to be told. But like any other illness, the diagnosis takes a bit of getting used to.

The key to understanding bipolar disorder is to do the research. Without education, you are just floundering around in a rough sea waiting to drown. And your friends and family will need to educate themselves, too, or they will not be able to help you. Support is paramount to your well being.

You will find that there is still a lot of stigma out there when it comes to bipolar disorder, and because of this you must learn who to share your diagnosis with. This book will help you decide.

I have reflected on my teenage years, when I was new to the diagnosis, and thought about everything I wanted to know. There was a lot I didn't understand, but when I was diagnosed back in the 1970s there wasn't a lot of help available.

The internet was not in common use back then. And there were no personal computers available for the everyday person. So I went to the library and read every book I could lay my hands on. This illness was called manic depression in those days and there was very little written about it.

Now, many years later, much research has been done. The name of the illness has been changed from manic depression to bipolar disorder and many new medications have been accepted by the FDA to treat it. When I was first diagnosed, Lithium was in common use. Now there are so many medications it is mind-blowing.

Looking back, I can see that my illness started at the death of my mother when I was 15, but I didn't get a diagnosis until I was twenty-five, so it went untreated until then. I suffered mainly with depression, so was given anti-depressants. These did not work too well because I didn't have major depressive disorder, I had bipolar disorder. Later, I was to find out that anti-depressants (especially the SSRIs) often bring on a manic reaction and this is what happened to me.

But now that you have a correct diagnosis, you are one step ahead and I can help you to understand your illness and show you what to do next.

This little book contains many checklists that you can fill in and add your own answers to. You can copy them out and put them in a journal or other safe place. Or you can keep them here in this book.

I will talk about every aspect of bipolar disorder with all the symptoms, warning signs and an action plan that you can take for bipolar episodes. I will tell you about the medications in use and other treatments such as the different kinds of therapies available and the lifestyle you need to establish in order to get well and stay well.

I will also talk about your triggers so that you will be aware of what is happening to you. This will enable you to lessen the symptoms or sometimes stop an episode in its tracks.

Wellness means different things to different people, so I shall ask you to deter-mine what it means to you. And I shall give you a Daily Wellness Plan that you can follow.

Further on in the book you will find coping skills, all about relationships and supporters, and at the end of the book, I shall give you an outline for a Crisis Plan should you get overwhelmed by the symptoms of bipolar.

At the very back of the book, you will find a list of books and articles you can read on the subject. The more you know about bipolar disorder the better.

One thing you should keep in mind is that many people with bipolar do very well and lead near normal lives. They have successful marriages and a prosperous career. In fact, I trained as a nurse and worked in the health industry for eleven years despite my diagnosis of bipolar 1.

I hope you enjoy this little book and start to feel confident that you can manage your bipolar disorder with ease.

What is Bipolar Disorder?

Bipolar disorder (previously called manic depression) is a severe mood disorder that adversely affects your thinking, behavior and energy.

Most people have varying moods as part of everyday life. They may feel down for a couple of days when things go wrong, and they may well refer to that as depression. But even though they feel down, their mood is nothing compared to the depression felt by someone with bipolar. Bipolar depression is more severe and disabling. It also lasts for an extended period of time and can result in a loss of functioning.

Bipolar depression makes you feel lethargic. You talk and move more slowly because you have little energy. You feel sad, guilty and worthless. You may want to isolate away from your friends and relatives.

With depression comes a total loss of motivation, even for things you once enjoyed. All you want to do is lie down on the couch and go to sleep.

If the depression continues to get worse, you will more than likely lose interest in everything around you and lie in bed all day. You won't have the energy to shower or even brush your teeth. When depression becomes severe you need emergency care.

Similarly, when someone says they are manic because they have had a few days of feeling extremely happy, that is not bipolar mania as they would feel ecstatic or irritable far beyond the normal everyday mood. They would need very little sleep (4 to 5 hours a night) yet not feel tired and have an enormous amount of energy. This can go on for weeks.

Bipolar mania is the opposite of depression. You suddenly find you have a lot to do and no time to do it. You may well take on various projects, be far more talkative than usual, indulge in risky behavior, and abuse various substances.

When mania or depression become severe the mood can escalate into psychosis causing you to hallucinate and experience delusions. This does not happen to everybody.

There is much publicity surrounding bipolar disorder these days, and people think it is more prevalent than it is. According to documented sources it affects approximately 5.7m adults, 2.8% of the population in America, and 45million people around the world.

There is no known cause for bipolar. Some scientists say it is genetic and there is certainly evidence of that. Others say it stems from childhood trauma, and yet others say it is a chemical imbalance in the brain. None of these theories have yet been proved, but medication and therapy are often given on the assumption that the chemical imbalance theory is correct. Sometimes these medications work, sometimes they do not.

Sadly, there is no known cure for bipolar disorder as it is a lifelong illness. But with medication and therapy it can be managed in order to cope with everyday life.

- Bipolar 1 disorder is when you have had at least one manic episode in your lifetime. It is not necessary to have had depression for a diagnosis of bipolar 1 to be made.

- Bipolar 2, on the other hand, is given when you have had repeated episodes of depression and at least one episode of hypomania which is like mania but less disabling.

There is still a great deal of stigma attached to bipolar disorder, and indeed to all mental illnesses. Depression seems to be more acceptable than bipolar disorder these days because people are ignorant of the symptoms of bipolar. Education is key.

CHAPTER ONE
SYMPTOMS

DEPRESSION

Most people with bipolar suffer from depression, except the few with bipolar 1 who have only manic mood swings.

As you probably know, bipolar depression is very difficult to live with and it can upset every part of your life. It can make your life unbearable. If you experience depression, you may notice it coming on over a few days to a few weeks, or you may wake up one morning feeling depressed. The rapid onset is especially true right after a manic episode subsides. Depressive episodes can last for days, weeks, or months making it difficult **to** function.

Unfortunately, without the proper treatment, depression can get worse until you are unable to function at all. So be diligent. At the first sign of depression, go to your doctor and let him or her prescribe some medication that can help you get well again.

People who have never been depressed have no understanding of what it feels like. It is useless trying to explain what it is like because unless you have experienced something yourself you will never be able to understand. It is just the same with a person who is blind. If this has not happened to you, you will not understand how it feels.

Your friends and relatives may be saying the wrong things to you, and some are particularly hurtful, but remember they do not understand what bipolar depression is really like. When you find a suitable article, print it out and give it to them to read. This can help them to understand your feelings when you are depressed.

Make sure you educate yourself by going online and reading everything you can about bipolar depression. It is essential to know all about your depressive symptoms if you have just received a diagnosis or if you have had bipolar for a long time.

You may recognize the symptoms of depression quite early on or you may only realize you are depressed after some time. Bipolar depression sometimes sneaks up on you and you don't realize it is happening.

Symptoms of Depression

Here are the common symptoms of depression. You can add your own symptoms at the bottom:

- ☐ Lethargy, feeling tired all the time.
- ☐ Unable to find the motivation to do anything, even things you once enjoyed.
- ☐ Unable to feel pleasure in anything, including sex
- ☐ Wanting to isolate, not answering the phone, texts or emails. Blocking people and not answering the door.
- ☐ Too tired to hold a conversation.
- ☐ Disturbances in sleeping, either insomnia or hypersomnia (sleeping all the time,)
- ☐ Changes in eating habits, eating far less or much more.
- ☐ Disturbances in weight.
- ☐ Feelings of worthlessness, guilt or sadness.
- ☐ Thinking of death and suicide all the time.
- ☐ Crying for no reason.

____

____

____

____

____

____

If this is you, be sure to discuss this with your doctor.

Warning Signs

Here are some warning signs of depression that you may recognize. You can check them off and add some of your own warning signs to the list:

- ☐ I quit cooking meals for myself.
- ☐ I don't tidy up the house.
- ☐ I want to eat chocolate all the time.
- ☐ People start to really annoy me.
- ☐ I start wondering why I don't have any friends.
- ☐ I can't sleep or sleep all day.
- ☐ I don't want to do anything at all.
- ☐ I hate everybody.
- ☐ I feel sad and irritable.
- ☐ I become very clumsy.
- ☐ I pick fights with people.
- ☐ I can't stop crying.
- ☐ I don't want to talk to anybody.
- ☐ I have no energy.
- ☐ I am thinking about suicide all the time.
- ☐ I feel very needy.
- ☐ My handwriting becomes very tiny.
- ☐ I don't want to shower.

____

____

____

____

Action Plan

- [ ] I can only do three things in one day.
- [ ] I need to take a nap.
- [ ] I can make a "to do" list and prioritize things.
- [ ] I can journal.
- [ ] I should really laugh at myself.
- [ ] I can sit in the sun.
- [ ] I need to accept that things are not good just now.
- [ ] I must go with the flow.
- [ ] I need to rest.
- [ ] I won't watch the news.
- [ ] I could fill in my Gratitude Journal.
- [ ] I can smile.
- [ ] I can breathe.
- [ ] I can play music or relax to videos.
- [ ] I must take baby steps.
- [ ] I could get out of the house.
- [ ] I could call a friend.

____

____

____

____

MANIA or HYPOMANIA

People with bipolar 1 have mania and people with bipolar 2 have hypomania. There is not much difference as far as the symptoms are concerned, but if you have hypomania, you may be able to function better than if you have mania. If you have bipolar 1, you often have to go to the hospital when manic, and treatment can be difficult.

People with hypomania (bipolar 2) are often very entertaining and they will find that other people are drawn to them. They are able to hold down a job, and with so much energy, they can get a lot done. On the other hand, if this should turn into mania (bipolar 1), things can escalate so fast that nothing gets done properly. This does not apply to everyone, of course, as there are many people with bipolar 1 who can hold down responsible jobs and live a very productive life.

In many ways mania is the exact opposite of depression. Instead of being tired and lethargic all the time, you feel on top of the world and have boundless energy. You may only need four or five hours sleep and can be awake at three in the morning scrubbing the grout in the kitchen tiles with a toothbrush.

The first flush of mania is often very exciting as you feel you could conquer the world. However, things can escalate very quickly, and, before you know it, you become very ill. It is not easy to stop mania in its tracks. It can be likened to a run away train that flies by the station.

Behavior becomes very irresponsible in hypomania and mania, and you take all kinds of risks that are out of character. Life savings can be lost at the casino in one night, road rage can kill, and relationships can be ruined altogether due to the volatile nature of mania and the promiscuity that often follows due to hyper-sexuality.

Mania can easily turn into irritability and anger, often due to thinking that other people are moving too slowly. Many things are said or done to people that you will regret when the mania subsides, and many people will lose their friends and relatives during a manic episode because people do not always forgive and forget.

The problem is when you are manic you do not understand that you are ill and may be very angry with other people who are trying to help you. Yet if you are to get well, you will need treatment as quickly as possible. It may mean adjusting your medications or it may mean spending time in the hospital.

Symptoms of Mania

The symptoms of mania are many and varied. Here are a few of them:

- [ ] Not needing much sleep.
- [ ] Talking very fast and loud.
- [ ] Veering off the subject and talking gibberish.
- [ ] Eating more or not eating at all.
- [ ] Ideas coming thick and fast.
- [ ] Getting angry with other people.
- [ ] Taking risks that you wouldn't normally take.
- [ ] Trying to do everything at once.
- [ ] Hyper-sexuality.

____

____

____

____

____

If you are having these symptoms, you will need to see your doctor. Try to accept what other people are telling you.

Warning Signs

The warning signs of mania are many and varied. See if you can recognize any of these and add others you may be experiencing to the list:

- ☐ I start reading five books at once.
- ☐ I take up new projects.
- ☐ I can't concentrate.
- ☐ I find myself talking very fast.
- ☐ I have many ideas coming into my head at once.
- ☐ I feel irritated all the time.
- ☐ I am hungry all the time.
- ☐ I get bored very quickly.
- ☐ I start spending too much money.
- ☐ Amazon suddenly becomes my new best friend.
- ☐ I have fits of temper.
- ☐ I am feeling ecstatically happy.
- ☐ I am flirting with the opposite sex.
- ☐ I feel benevolent feelings towards everyone.
- ☐ I do large, loopy handwriting.

Action Plan

- ☐ I should STOP and breathe.
- ☐ I can say a mantra over and over again.
- ☐ I must slow down.
- ☐ I should take some days off work.
- ☐ I should try to lie down and take a nap.
- ☐ I should think twice before making sexual passes at strangers.
- ☐ I should stop spending money.
- ☐ I could put my credit cards in the bank for safe keeping.
- ☐ I need to believe people when they say I am ill.
- ☐ I should see my doctor.

PSYCHOSIS

Unfortunately, severe mania or depression can lead to psychosis for people with bipolar 1. Fortunately, the psychosis experienced by people with bipolar 1 is only temporary unlike that experienced by people with schizophrenia, but the symptoms are the same. For anyone who has had psychosis they will know that it can be very disturbing indeed. People with bipolar 2 occasionally experience psychosis but it is more prevalent in bipolar 1.

There is a very fine line between severe mania or severe depression and psychosis, so it is difficult for you or anyone else to realize that things have changed. This becomes apparent, though, if you should become paranoid and involve other people.

Psychosis means a break with reality. It is no longer easy to understand what is real and what is not.

If you have psychosis, you will likely experience hallucinations and delusions, and sometimes, you will be paranoid and unable to listen to reason. This is because psychosis is not a logical state, so nothing makes any sense. A world with hallucinations and delusions can be very confusing and frightening. Yet some people can function fairly well even though they are psychotic.

Hallucinations usually affect the senses. It is not uncommon to hear your name being called when there is nobody there, or to smell smoke or other strange smells in the house or feel strange things creeping over your skin. Certain foods taste metallic or like blood, and you can see all kinds of weird shapes and animals that aren't there.

Delusions are very common, the most prevalent being delusions of grandeur, thinking that you are Jesus Christ or the only person in the world who knows the cure for cancer. It is not uncommon to think you are being followed by a member of the CIA, or the neighbors have bugged your walls and are listening to everything you say. Because delusions seem so real, it is usually impossible to convince a psychotic person that they are not.

Psychosis can be mood-congruent or mood-incongruent. If you have mood-congruent symptoms, they will reflect or exaggerate the mood you are in. Mood-incongruent symptoms are the exact opposite and contradict your present mood.

Mood stabilizers or anti-psychotics may well be prescribed by your doctor as they have had a lot of success in treating bipolar psychosis. If your symptoms are uncontrollable or if you have mood-incongruent psychosis, you may well be admitted to the hospital. ECT (electroconvulsive therapy) can be used as a last resort if medications are not effective. It is also a good idea to do some family therapy or talk therapy in order to discover what is real and what is not.

Symptoms of Psychosis

Symptoms of psychosis include:

- [ ] Isolation.
- [ ] Jumbled thoughts.
- [ ] Rambling, or hard to follow speech.
- [ ] Hallucinations.
- [ ] Delusions.
- [ ] Paranoia.
- [ ] Not wanting to be touched.

____

____

____

____

____

____

Warning Signs

There are many warning signs with psychosis, but they are sometimes so vague that they go unrecognized. Here are a few of them:

- [ ] I have obsessions about things.
- [ ] I am seeing, hearing, feeling and smelling things that are not there.
- [ ] I think people are talking about me.
- [ ] Things disappear, then reappear.
- [ ] I have irrational responses to things people do or say.
- [ ] I feel spaced out most of the time.
- [ ] I do not trust the system.
- [ ] I say crazy things.
- [ ] Billboards seem to be talking about me.
- [ ] I think people have stolen from me.
- [ ] I am sure my room is bugged.
- [ ] I have strange feelings as if I am in a dream or in a play.
- [ ] I feel I am unattached to my body.
- [ ] I have totally lost interest in anything.

____

____

____

____

____

____

____

Action Plan

It is difficult to have an action plan because most people stop being aware of the real world when they have psychosis. If you have a gap in your psychotic thinking, you can do these things:

- ☐ I need to STOP what I am doing.
- ☐ I must check my thoughts to see if they are rational.
- ☐ I need to find some help from my doctor or my family.

MIXED FEATURES

Most people think of bipolar as an illness with highs and lows. They liken it to being on a roller coaster with moods alternating between mania and depression over a lifetime.

While this is true much of the time, you can actually have both symptoms of depression and symptoms of mania either at the same time or in quick succession. This means you can go from euphoria to despair in a matter of moments.

Symptoms of psychosis can also occur at the same time as depression and mania, further complicating the diagnosis and treatment.

This used to be called bipolar disorder with mixed episodes but has now changed to bipolar disorder with mixed features. It is quite common and can affect a third to a half of the people with a bipolar diagnosis.

When you have mixed features you may have serious disturbances in mood and this can be quite serious and difficult to treat. It is essential to see your doctor early in the process as it can take a while to recover. Therapy is also helpful.

Symptoms of Mixed Features

Symptoms of bipolar disorder with mixed features are:

- ☐ Features of mania and depression at the same time or in close succession.
- ☐ Interrupted sleep.
- ☐ Disturbances in appetite.
- ☐ Jumbled thoughts.
- ☐ Rapid speech.
- ☐ Crying.
- ☐ Psychotic features.

Warning Signs

Here are some of the warning signs of mixed features.

- ☐ I feel extreme agitation.
- ☐ I have racing thoughts.
- ☐ I find it difficult to make decisions.
- ☐ I want to climb out of my skin.
- ☐ I can't stop chewing my lips.
- ☐ I can't relax.
- ☐ I can't catch my breath.
- ☐ I feel sick and have stomach pains.
- ☐ I am very worried about money.
- ☐ I am scared of the future.
- ☐ I feel suicidal.
- ☐ I can't think clearly.

Action Plan

An action plan may be difficult to follow because your thinking is off, but you can try these things:

- ☐ I need to sit down and relax.
- ☐ My breathing is shallow so I should do some breathing exercises.
- ☐ I should make a "to do" list.
- ☐ I should get help.
- ☐ I must call my doctor.

TRIGGERS

As you may know, your illness probably does not come out of nowhere. We all have things that cause our moods to change. You are going along quite nicely for a few days, then another mood swing takes over and all is lost once again. This is soul-destroying and puts you at the mercy of your moods. It lets them take the lead and have complete power over you.

It is true that sometimes we seem to get ill for no reason, but if you look hard enough at what has taken place in the past few days, you are likely to find that something or the other has triggered your mood and made you ill.

This is why it is a good idea to document your moods. You can print out mood charts online. There are many websites that have them. Some are just for mood swings, but many have things like the medicine you take, the time you go to bed, and the things that you are doing before the mood swing took over. You can also make your own mood chart to suit your particular situation.

Now that you know you are not powerless where your moods are concerned it is time for you to look at what triggers your illness and how you react to certain things. You can do this in a journal, or you can add your triggers to the list below:

Triggers That Cause Mood Swings

- ☐ Not doing my Daily Wellness Plan. (To follow)
- ☐ Insomnia.
- ☐ Chaos in your environment.
- ☐ Multi-tasking.
- ☐ Exhaustion.
- ☐ Financial problems.
- ☐ Things breaking down.
- ☐ Physical problems.
- ☐ Loneliness.
- ☐ Bright lights.
- ☐ Crowds.
- ☐ Noise.
- ☐ Death in the family, divorce, having a baby.
- ☐ Being around toxic people.
- ☐ Fearful of the future.
- ☐ Being criticized.
- ☐ Feeling left out.
- ☐ Being judged.
- ☐ Feeling overwhelmed.
- ☐ Feeling invisible.
- ☐ Too much to do.
- ☐ Paperwork.
- ☐ Having no friends.
- ☐ Coming out of the hospital.

____

____

____

____

CHAPTER TWO
TREATMENT

MEDICATIONS

When you get a diagnosis of bipolar disorder, you will no doubt be prescribed
a medication, or maybe more than one if the doctor aims to treat all your symptoms
at once. Taking medication may not be something you want to do, but it will
more than likely make you feel much better.

Many people resist medication and stay ill or even get worse. That is not what
you need when you have a serious mood disorder. Some people refuse to take medication at all, then they get sicker and often end up in the hospital. Then there are
others who say they don't need medication because they are feeling much better.
What they don't realize is that it is the medication that is making them feel better.
So, it is worth taking what the doctor has prescribed and getting well again.

Sadly, not all medications work for all people and there are side effects. Most of
the time, these side effects are not serious and will go away in a short space of
time. If they are bothering you, you should let your doctor know. Serious side
effects are rare but should be reported to your doctor immediately. I am not
going to give you a long list of side effects here as it is best that you do that
research yourself. All medications have side effects, even Aspirin.

When you get your prescription, be sure to ask your doctor about any side effects, then when you get home look up the medicine online to understand what it
is. **Do not skip this step.** It is very wise to learn all about your medication. Your
doctor will appreciate your interest.

Sometimes, it takes a long time to get your medications right as the doctor has to
prescribe a different medication for each part of your illness. He may prescribe
a mood stabilizer or two to counteract the frequency of mania or depression,
an anti-depressant for your depression and something else for your anxiety. The
only thing you can do is to be patient while this is happening.

Here is a list of all the most common medications. You can check off the medication the doctor has given you and research it further. Don't forget to ask him
if the medication has side effects while you are in his office. Then you will know
what to expect.

MOOD-STABILIZERS

Lithium
divalproex sodium (Depakote)
lamotrigine (Lamictal)
Valproic acid (Depakene)
Carbamazepine (Equetro)
Topiramate (Topamax)

ANTI-PSYCHOTIC MEDICATIONS

olanzapine (Zyprexa)
risperidone (Risperdal)
quetiapine (Seroquel)
asenapine (Saphris)

ANTI-DEPRESSANT MEDICATIONS

SNRI's (Serotonin-norepinephrine reuptake inhibitors)

levomilnacipran (Fetazima)
duloxetine (Cymbalta, Yentreve)
venlafaxine (Effexor)

SSRIs (Selective serotonine reuptake inhibitors)

atalopram (Celexa)
fluvoxamine (Luvox)
escitalopram (Lexapro)
fluoxetine (Prozac)
parnexetine (Paxil)
sertraline (Zoloft)

(Tricyclics & tetracyclists)

clomipramine (Anafranil)
amitriptyline (Elavil)
desipramite (Norpramin)
imipramine (Norpramin)
nortriptyline (Pamelor)

(MAOIs)

phenelzine (Nardil)
tranylcypromine (Parnate)

ANXIETY MEDICATIONS

diazepam (Valium)
alprazolam (Xanex)
clonazepam (Klonepin)

THERAPY

Many people, including psychiatrists, believe that therapy is a major part of getting well when you have bipolar disorder. But it is true that sometimes therapy is hard to come by. You may not have a suitable therapist in your town, or the fees may be out of your reach. If something is available for you, it is advisable that you take advantage of it. Many therapists use a sliding scale so that you can afford to pay, and churches and other religious institutions often provide therapy for a nominal amount.

There are many types of therapy, and it is sometimes difficult to choose which one is right for you, so I have written a brief description of the more popular ones below. You may like a structured type of therapy like CBT (cognitive behavioral therapy) or DBT (dialectical behavioral therapy) or you may prefer to just talk with a person who has experience with you illness.

Most therapists practice the type of therapy they were trained to use, although those who have been in practice for a while tend to use a conglomeration of different therapies at once.

Here is a short list of the different types of therapy so that you can make an informed choice:

CBT

CBT is a very common form of talk therapy. It is used for many mental health problems including bipolar disorder. In fact, it is often recommended for bipolar disorder, usually along with medication.

The limited number of sessions are very structured and teach you how to become aware of your inappropriate or negative reactions to challenging situations. It also helps you develop self-confidence in your everyday life and encourages you to step out of your comfort zone which is particularly useful if you have anxiety. (Almost half the people with bipolar disorder have some form of anxiety.)

CBT produces quick results and there is scientific evidence that it is effective in improving your quality of life. There are no health risks as such, except that you might feel uncomfortable, especially at first, when you are learning about the therapy. Homework is usually given between sessions.

DBT

Based on CBT, DBT is another form of talk therapy. It was developed in the '70s by Marsha Lineham and was used extensively in borderline personality disorder (BDP) but is now used in many mental illness including bipolar disorder, PTSD, and suicidal behavior.

DBT works on your negative or intense emotional reactions to everyday stimulus, and teaches you better ways of coping. It helps you accept that your present way of coping is causing you unnecessary problems and there are ways to stay calm in challenging situations.

DBT teaches healthy ways of relating to other people and dealing with the everyday stress of modern life. You are taught mindfulness skills which help you stay calm.

TALK THERAPY

Many people prefer talk therapy (psychotherapy) as opposed to a more structured type of therapy. You are able to tell your story and relate to a professional person who can help you overcome your challenges.

It can be difficult opening up at first, and a lot of people have trouble talking about their emotions, but if you persist, you can get a great deal of support in talk therapy.

Talk therapy may take weeks or maybe years in which time you build up a relationship with your therapist. This can be especially useful for people with bipolar disorder as they need stability in their lives. Many people say that bipolar disorder needs to be treated with medication and therapy for a long time.

GROUP THERAPY

Group therapy is a form of psychotherapy involving one or more mental health facilitators and two or more people. Many groups comprise eight to twelve people who come together to talk in a safe and supportive place.

There are several types of group therapy: CBT groups, Interpersonal groups, Psychoeducational groups, skills development groups, and support groups. Groups are either open or closed by invitation only. It is usually more affordable than individual therapy.

Chairs are often arranged in a circle so that participants and facilitators can see each other and their reactions to situations that are discussed. If you are going to do group therapy, you must be willing to share your experiences with the group and often give feedback to others. It can be very helpful to see how others manage situations that you have difficulty with. When you see how others are coping, it teaches you that it is possible to cope well in many situations.

As people with bipolar find it hard to form friendships, it is a good thing to form relationships with people in these groups. You will find you can meet them after group and enjoy things together that you might not experience alone.

CHAPTER THREE
LIFESTYLE

LIFESTYLE

As you now know, it is advisable to take medication and do therapy if you have bipolar disorder. These two things are very important and will help with your mood swings, but they are not all you can do. It takes a few minutes to swallow your medication, and an hour or so to do therapy, but that leaves many hours in the week when you could be working on yourself. This means you need to strive for a healthy lifestyle and be sure you are doing things that will help you get well. You cannot rely on a little tablet to do all the work. You need to take some responsibility yourself.

It is good to remember that you are not helpless when it comes to bipolar disorder. There are many things you can do to experience a better quality of life. Only you can make healthy choices, but they can make all the difference to your situation. Never lose hope with bipolar disorder. You are in control of how you run your life.

It is often said that managing bipolar disorder is a full-time job. There is some truth in this because if you lead an unhealthy lifestyle you need to work very hard to stabilize your mood swings. Fortunately, there are many things you can do to help yourself get well and stay well.

Here is a short list of things you can try:

- ☐ Get a good night's sleep.
- ☐ Eat a healthy diet.
- ☐ Do some exercise.
- ☐ Stick to a routine.
- ☐ Do some relaxation exercises.
- ☐ Think positive thoughts.
- ☐ Avoid alcohol and drugs.

____

____

SLEEP

Possibly the most important thing after medication and therapy for bipolar disorder is sleep. Mood disorders affect your sleeping. You either can't get to sleep, wake up in the night, or wake up too early in the morning. You may also experience the opposite of this, especially when you are depressed. You find you cannot stop sleeping and sleep for twelve to eighteen hours a day. This is called hypersomnia and is very common in bipolar depression.

Sometimes you need a little help in order to get into a regular sleep pattern. Melatonin (over the counter) is good in small doses and has no side effects. Be sure to clear all over the counter and herbal supplements with your doctor before taking them to avoid any harmful interactions. If you find that you still can't sleep, your psychiatrist may be able to prescribe something to help. Often anti-depressants work for this.

There are several things you can do to promote a healthy sleep routine:

- ☐ Go to bed and get up at the same time each night.
- ☐ Keep the bedroom dark and quiet.
- ☐ Save the bedroom for sleep and sex only.
- ☐ Turn off all devices.
- ☐ Avoid strenuous exercise just before bedtime.
- ☐ Do some relaxation exercises.
- ☐ Avoid caffeine and alcohol just before bedtime as well.
- ☐ Take a warm bath to promote sleep.
- ☐ Drink a warm, milky drink.

____

____

____

DIET

The saying, "We are what we eat" is so true when it comes to bipolar disorder. Our bodies and brains need certain nutrients that keep us healthy. Sometimes, these are difficult to come by due to inconvenience or financial considerations, but it will help you get well if you do try to eat healthy food.

Eating well can take a bit of planning and not everybody has the inclination or the time to spend on getting a meal together. This definitely applies when you are having a depressive episode as you have no energy or inclination to cook. It is tempting to eat junk food because it is easy to come by and requires little to no cooking, but in the end it is not healthy. Existing on junk food makes you feel bad and can make your illness worse.

Here are some things you can try:

- ☐ Aim to eat at least two healthy meals a day.
- ☐ Avoid processed foods and junk foods.
- ☐ Shop on the periphery of the store.
- ☐ Avoid too many carbohydrates.
- ☐ Eat some omega 3 fatty acids found in oily fish and nuts.
- ☐ Eat protein found in meats and dairy produce.
- ☐ Drink Boost or Ensure.

EXERCISE

I am sure you have heard that exercise is good for you. You may not like exercise, and that is understandable, but exercise is helpful in making you feel well. Even a short ten-minute walk a day is good for you and it gets you out into the fresh air.

If you can manage it, take out a gym membership and try to keep to a schedule. It is also good to get out of the house, especially when depressed, and socialize if you are able. You may think exercise is the very last thing you want to do when you are depressed, and I can understand that, but if it will make you feel better, I am sure you will think it is necessary. Also exercise produces endorphins in the brain which give you a sense of well-being.

Here are some things you can do:

- [ ] Take a short walk several times a week.
- [ ] Cycle.
- [ ] Swim.
- [ ] Lift weights.
- [ ] Go to the gym.
- [ ] Play a team sport.
- [ ] Run.

ROUTINE

A routine is something you do every day. Schedules are things like appointments and do not necessarily come at the same time every day or every week.

You can try to adopt a routine in the morning, getting the kids off to school or going to work, but whatever it is, people with bipolar disorder seem to have difficulties maintaining a routine.

It is natural, when you think about it, that people who are having irregular mood swings are out of balance and a routine is the last thing they want to think about. Yet a routine is very valuable to help you control your mood swings because you know you should be doing certain things every day no matter what your mood.

In order to keep to a routine, you need to make it simple to follow with very few steps. If you make it complicated, you are less likely to stick to it. I suggest you write your routine down in a journal or put a sticky note on the fridge or the bathroom mirror where you can see it every day. This will be a good reminder and will help you keep track of what you should be doing next.

RELAXATION EXERCISES

Bipolar disorder is hard to live with and you can get to the stage of exhaustion very quickly. With exhaustion comes lethargy and not wanting to do anything. This is unhelpful behavior and will make you feel worse over time.

This is why you need to take time out to do some relaxation exercises every day. Make a habit of it. You don't need to spend more than a few minutes relaxing. Even ten minutes of concentrated effort is well worth your while. Spend ten minutes lying down with your eyes closed and listening to soft music or do some deep breathing exercises or visualization. You might like to try yoga or qi gong as both promote relaxation. What ever you do, make it part of your routine. You can check it off on your mood chart or in your journal. And you can make it part of your routine.

POSITIVE THOUGHTS

If you have bipolar depression, I can guarantee that you have negative thoughts in your head. And it is these negative thoughts that keep you from getting well again. It is so easy to think negatively when you are ill because everything is such an effort, and this gives you a chance to chastise yourself.

Negative thoughts come in all shapes and sizes, but most of them are scolding you for doing, or not doing, what your mind tells you. This entails a string of accusatory thoughts, telling you over and over that you are worthless, hopeless, helpless and guilty of all the things that have happened in your life. These thoughts rumble round in your brain all day and you think them over and over again. The same old tape runs in your mind and causes a lot of suffering. The little voice in your head says:

> "You are so lazy."
> "You are fat and stupid."
> "You can't get anything right."
> "You are worthless, and nobody cares about you."

When this is happening to you, you take it all in and believe it. Yet thinking it doesn't make it true. When you feel better you will be able to see that the little voice in your head lies. The little voice wants to make you feel bad.

If you are thinking these things, it is a good idea to get therapy in one form or another. Then you can discuss it with somebody who understands. Cognitive behavioral therapy (CBT) is designed to catch these negative thoughts and turn them around, but even talk therapy can help you catch these lies.

ALCOHOL AND DRUGS

Many people with bipolar disorder also have an addiction to alcohol and/or drugs. This is called dual-diagnosis, and it is very difficult to deal with. Although drinking alcohol can make you feel better for a while, it is not recommended with bipolar medications, and it also interrupts your sleep. If you can avoid alcohol and drugs, so much the better. But if you are unable, do see your doctor and let him help you.

When you have bipolar disorder, you should monitor your lifestyle. This means that you will not be able to drink and stay out all night at parties with your friends. You need your sleep for one thing, and you want your medications to work. You will quickly find out who your friends are when some help you out with your illness while others encourage you to drink. It is not nice to have to leave a party before anyone else, but if it can save you from an episode, it is well worth it.

CHAPTER FOUR
WELLNESS

GETTING WELL AND STAYING WELL

Now that we have talked about the various ways you can get well, let's look at how it actually feels to be well. You may not be able to see that you could ever get well when you have a serious mood disorder, but nothing could be further from the truth. Many people with bipolar disorder do get well and stay well. That is a good goal to work towards.

You might like to think about this or make some notes in your journal. You could even do some free thinking when lying down to relax. Just let the mind wander and ask yourself what wellness means to you.

Wellness is not the same for everybody as many people have disabilities besides bipolar disorder that they have to contend with. When this is the case, it is hard to think of being well. So, if this is you, it is best to concentrate on the things you are able to do and not worry about the rest.

Here are some thoughts about wellness. You can add to this list if you wish:

- [ ] Staying in control.
- [ ] Having accountability.
- [ ] Feeling happy.
- [ ] Staying engaged in your goal to get well.
- [ ] Staying true to yourself.
- [ ] Seeing a bright future.
- [ ] Enjoying life.
- [ ] Eating healthy.
- [ ] Having fun.
- [ ] Having a desire to get well.
- [ ] Having a good support group.
- [ ] Being surrounded by love.
- [ ] Looking forward to the next day.
- [ ] Not living in the past.

HOW I FEEL WHEN I AM WELL

When you are in the depths of depression, it may seem as if you are always ill and will remain ill. When depressed, it is difficult to focus on positive things and you forget what you are like when you are well. But wellness does occur in between the various episodes, and it pays to remember that. It is easy to become disheartened when you are very ill, but there is always hope and with hope you can climb any mountain.

Strangely enough, when you are having a manic episode you don't feel ill at all. In fact, you can balk at the suggestion. This makes it very difficult for others to help you and the mania can escalate if you are not careful.

Many people have months in between episodes when they are their normal selves. This is called a euthymic period and it is a big relief from all the mood swings.

So, bear that in mind. You will not always be ill. Work towards being well again.

Here is a list of the type of things you can jot down about how you feel when you are well. It is a great idea to have this list handy as you can look at it when you are ill and realize that you don't always feel like that. Keep it somewhere safe or write your answers down here.

This is what I feel like when I am well:

- [ ] Cheerful.
- [ ] Grounded.
- [ ] Optimistic.
- [ ] Hopeful.
- [ ] Energetic.
- [ ] Strong.
- [ ] Sociable.
- [ ] Connected.
- [ ] Ambitious.
- [ ] Present.
- [ ] Focused.
- [ ] Mindful.
- [ ] Worthy.
- [ ] Competent.
- [ ] Responsible.
- [ ] Joyful.
- [ ] Balanced.
- [ ] Calm.
- [ ] Confident.
- [ ] Grateful.
- [ ] Blessed.

____

____

____

____

____

THINGS I CAN DO TO STAY WELL

Now that you know what you are like when you are well, you need to think about the things you can do to stay well. It is no good getting well only to relapse immediately although, unfortunately, this does sometimes happen.

Paying attention to your triggers can save you from a mood swing. That is why it is very important to have all your triggers written down for when you need them. It is so easy to get caught up with what you are doing that you don't realize what is happening. But if you have your triggers written down, you should be able to see that you are reacting badly.

If at all possible, you need to work on your reaction to things. If you are the type of person who flies off the handle when things go wrong a manic mood swing may be just around the corner. Mania is not always made up of positive things, sometimes negativity and anger are the responses that you get. Mania is likely to follow a few bad nights if you have bipolar disorder, so you need to pay careful attention to your sleep hygiene.

On the other hand, bad news may put you into a depressed state quite easily. You hear some bad news and immediately dwell upon it to the exclusion of everything else. When you ruminate like this, depression can easily follow. You start to feel sad, hopeless and worthless over night, then before you know it you are very ill with depression.

Here are some things you can do to stay well:

- [ ] Take your medications.
- [ ] Watch comedies.
- [ ] Pray.
- [ ] Keep the house clean and tidy.
- [ ] Make the bed as soon as you get up.
- [ ] Do deep breathing.
- [ ] Stay sober.
- [ ] Do positive self-talk.
- [ ] Be kind to yourself.
- [ ] Go to a support group.
- [ ] Play with your pets.
- [ ] Keep in touch with family and friends.
- [ ] Read a book.
- [ ] Go out for a coffee with a friend.
- [ ] Go to a movie.
- [ ] Try something new.
- [ ] Be creative.

Get dressed when you first get up so that you don't get depressed as easily.

COPING SKILLS

Despite all your efforts to stay well, sometimes life just happens and before you know it you are feeling sick again. Any number of things can go wrong in a day, or perhaps you have something very important happening in your life. Divorces happen, people have accidents, and people die. These things are a part of life and there is very little you can do to control them. But these are the times when you need to be extra vigilant. You know you have an illness, and you can't afford to take more time off work or be unable to look after the children. You have to remain as well as possible.

This is where your coping skills come in. If you have a list at the ready for when things go wrong, you will be more likely to stay well. People use all manner of coping skills, so study them and be creative as you develop your own. It is very useful to have a list handy that you can refer to when times are bad.

- ☐ Keep in touch with your friends.
- ☐ Talk to your support group.
- ☐ Meditate.
- ☐ Yoga.
- ☐ Qi Gong.
- ☐ Use aromatherapy/essential oils.
- ☐ Take a bubble bath.
- ☐ Do some gardening.
- ☐ Journal.
- ☐ Take a nature walk.
- ☐ Listen to music.
- ☐ Light candles.
- ☐ Give someone a hug.
- ☐ Go to a meeting.
- ☐ See your therapist.

☐ Use lists.
☐ Maintain a time management system.
☐ Do the worst things first.
☐ Learn to say, "No."
☐ Delegate.
☐ Don't get distracted – just do it.
☐ Talk to someone.
☐ Be creative.
☐ Do some exercise.
☐ Make a nice meal.

CHAPTER FIVE
DAILY WELLNESS PLAN

DAILY WELLNESS PLAN

It is difficult to keep up with all the things you should be doing to stay well with bipolar. But the fact is, if you want to get well and stay well you need to treat bipolar disorder like a full-time job.

For this reason, you need a Daily Wellness Plan that you can copy and put on the fridge or in your journal. It is always good to have it nearby so that you can stick to it every day.

If you find that you cannot do everything on the plan, don't worry. We all have lapses. Just do the best you can and even if you only do half of it, you should see signs of improvement.

- [ ] Go to bed and get up at the same time every day.
- [ ] Stick to your morning routine.
- [ ] Take your medication as directed by the doctor.
- [ ] Keep in touch with your doctor and therapist.
- [ ] Eat a nutritious diet.
- [ ] Eat at regular mealtimes.
- [ ] Use your journal.
- [ ] Check in with how you are feeling each day:
    - [ ] Physically
    - [ ] Mentally
    - [ ] Emotionally
- [ ] Connect with others.
- [ ] Sit in the sun for 15 minutes a day.
- [ ] Drink plenty of water.
- [ ] Do something creative.
- [ ] Do some form of exercise.
- [ ] Do something for fun.

CHAPTER SIX
WHAT OTHERS CAN DO TO HELP

STIGMA

Whether we like it or not, the fact is that in many cases bipolar disorder is not acceptable to the public at large. There is no point in denying it. Stigma is alive and well.

In recent years, a lot has changed for people with depression only (major depressive disorder.) At one time this was a taboo illness as well, but it is now openly discussed without fear of reprisals. Not so with bipolar disorder. Of course, this is not fair, but that is the way it is.

The fact is other people are afraid of things they don't understand. They either think it is contagious (yes!) or something they may have in their family. Nobody wants it in their family, that is obvious. They may also think the person with bipolar is dangerous, especially due to the inferences that people with bipolar are responsible for mass shootings. This couldn't be further from the truth as people with bipolar are far more likely to be docile than they are aggressive, but that is not how the public sees it.

As I have said, people are more accepting of depression, but mania is another thing entirely. Even by its name it is stigmatizing. People just do not understand mania at all. It is doubtful if you can understand it yourself! But nevertheless, mania is part of the illness and cannot be ignored.

Mania is very unpredictable, and the person is highly likely to take major risks. They are also likely to say mean things to the very people who could possibly help them, and get ostracized in the process.

But whatever the reason for the stigma it is very hurtful. You may well find that people are talking about you behind your back. Others will just ignore you altogether. Whatever the reaction, it is very painful for the person with the illness. No other illness causes a person to change their whole personality like bipolar does. Bipolar is not a character or personality defect. It is an illness that is treatable with medication and therapy.

When someone is in a crisis situation, they are very likely to be misunderstood by the police as mental health education is sorely lacking in the police force.

SPEAKING OUT

Should you tell other people that you have bipolar disorder?

This is a very personal decision, but you should take time to think it through with each and every relationship you have. People react differently to news like this, and some people will accept it whereas other people will not.

If you are one of the lucky ones, you will have a family who is understanding. They may even stand by you and do things to help. They may be a shoulder to cry on and be there for you in the event of a crisis situation. That is the ideal scenario.

But sadly, not everybody is so lucky. People they thought would understand do not, and they either make this very clear or just leave you to it. You can never tell what reaction you are going to get from speaking out and telling the truth.

Friends are an unknown quantity as well. People you thought would understand, or at least be able to help you when times get tough, suddenly do not want to know, and break off the friendship. It can be quite a surprise and very hurtful indeed. However, some friends can be very helpful. People are all different.

Telling your boss or your colleagues can open up a can of worms. People talk and you are bound to get someone who talks about you behind your back. Before you know it, people are ignoring you or deliberately avoiding you. Sometimes, it is a good thing to tell your boss. They may well be able to arrange time off for you when you get sick, but other times it can cost you your job.

You may be one of those people who are determined to be up front with everybody you meet. There are many people with bipolar who operate like that these days. But whatever happens, you must take responsibility for it yourself.

As I say, it is a personal decision, one that nobody else can make for you.

SUPPORT SYSTEM

Now that you have digested the fact that not everybody is your friend when it comes to bipolar disorder, you will need to think about the people who will stand by you and support you when you are sick. There are always people who will understand and be helpful. You need to seek them out carefully.

You will usually find that the people who are supportive are those who have some understanding of the illness. These are the people who have familiarized themselves with bipolar disorder. They will not think it is an easy illness to manage, but they will understand that with the right care it can be done. These are the people who will willingly stand by you when times get tough. Ignorance is not bliss when it comes to something as serious as bipolar disorder.

It is often wise to help these supportive people better understand the illness for themselves. You can do this by printing out some literature and asking them to read it. There are also many books on the subject, or you can let them read this little book. They will probably be grateful for your efforts.

However, you should make a list of your supporters. It could be a short list, shorter than you had hoped for, and certainly not ideal. But if you are lucky, you will have a long list of supporters to help you cope when you are ill.

Here are a few suggestions for your list:

- ☐ Family doctor.
- ☐ Psychiatrist.
- ☐ Therapist.
- ☐ Local clinic.
- ☐ Support Groups.
- ☐ Various members of your family.
- ☐ National Support Groups.
- ☐ Crisis Line – 988.
- ☐ Friends.
- ☐ Colleagues.

It is a good idea to get certain people together to discuss the support you will need and to educate them with suitable literature. It would also be wise to have a Crisis Plan to give to them for times when you are unable to help yourself.

You may well find that people really do want to help. In that case, it is best to have some idea of the ways they can help, and be prepared to tell them. You may need somebody to take you to the doctor's or make an appointment for you. You may also need someone to cook you a meal, look after the children or do some housework. People are often very willing to help, so be sure to tell them what they can do for you. And there is no shame in asking for help. Most of us hate asking for help. But when you need it, it is quite acceptable to ask.

CRISIS PLAN

As with the Daily Wellness Plan that we discussed before, you will want to keep your Crisis Plan handy so that if and when the time comes that you need it, you can go to it yourself or have your supporters use it and take over your care.

When you have bipolar, it is sometimes difficult to focus when you are in crisis. Your mind is either all over the place or shuts down completely and you are unable to think clearly. Your brain feels as if it is full of cotton wool. This is hardly surprising because a crisis situation can come on so quickly you are not prepared for it.

It is a good idea to make your Crisis Plan easily accessible. As with the Daily Wellness Plan it is good to copy this out and put it in your journal. Otherwise, you can put it on your fridge. Just make sure you can go to it if necessary.

The plan will have concise instructions as to your wishes so people will be in no doubt as to what you need. If you or the police decide that you would be better off in the hospital, it is a good idea to have everything ready beforehand.

- You may like to pack a small carry-on bag so that you can just pick it up if you should need to go to the hospital. It is very difficult to think what you should wear when your thoughts are whirling round in your head. Some hospitals do not let you wear your own clothes until the doctor approves it, but it is useful to have your own clothes there for later.

- Make sure you have a list of all your medications, both prescription medications and over-the-counter vitamins and minerals. Add the dosage and the time of the day that you should take them. You do not need to take medications with you if you are going to the hospital.

- Keep a list of all your doctors – your family doctor and your psychiatrist, and any other doctor who may be involved in your care. Put their addresses and phone numbers on your list.

- Also don't forget to add your therapist/s name, address and phone number to this list.

- Make a list of all your supporters with their addresses and telephone numbers.

- Have a list of the hospitals or care centers you would be willing to go to, and those you do not want to go to.

- Also, make a list of the things that you do not want like ECT, solitary confinement and restraints.

At least, when you have completed this list, you will be able to put your mind at rest and know that you have something to work on should the time come for others to take over your care.

I know it is not nice to think that you will ever need this list, but it is better to be safe than sorry.

In Conclusion

I hope you have enjoyed this little book on how to take care of your bipolar disorder. It is handy to have a simple guide when you are first diagnosed or even when you have had bipolar for a long time rather than read a full-length book.

Also, I hope that it has been useful to you and that you filled in all the empty boxes in the check lists throughout this book. It is very important that you have this information on hand as bipolar disorder can sneak up on you and it doesn't wait until you are ready for it.

Now that you have your list of triggers, you should be able to reach for it and see that if you are not careful a new episode will follow. Hopefully, you will be free of bipolar for a long time. This is my wish for you.

As always, bipolar is a difficult illness to manage but it can be done. Many people live full and happy lives, keeping a family together and holding down a career. Even if you are not able to do this, you can always pat yourself on the back for the way you are coping and hope that things will improve shortly.

It has been a pleasure writing this little book for you. It has helped me better hone my own thoughts and is always handy should my bipolar disorder return. As I have said, bipolar is not curable, nor does it stay away forever. No matter how well you are, you may be revisited by this illness when you least expect it.

I have been 100% well for the past three years, but I attribute that to taking my medications, doing therapy and living a healthy lifestyle. In the past two years, I have written four books on bipolar disorder and one on loneliness. I have also written a book of poetry. They are all available on Amazon.

Bipolar is always about hope. I wish you well in the future.

Resources

My Books:

"How to Live with Bipolar"
"Bipolar 1 Disorder Rescue Plan"
"37 Symptoms of Bipolar Depression" (workbook)
"The Bipolar Disorder Guide"

Books by other people:

"The Bipolar Disorder Survival Guide" by David Miklowitz, PhD
"Understanding Bipolar Disorder: The Essential Family Guide by Aimee Daramus
"Mad Like Me: Travels in Bipolar Country" by Merryl Hammond PhD

Podcasts

Apple podcasts: Psych Central: Inside Bipolar by Gabe & Dr. Nichole – 42 episodes
Spotify: The Bipolar Disorder Family by Bipolar Bob
Spotify: Life with Bipolar Disorder by James A. Heaton

YouTube

Dr. Tracey Marks (mental disorders)

My other non-bipolar books

"A Practical Guide to Overcoming Loneliness"
"We Never Did Mornings" (poetry)

Author Bio

Sally Alter is a prolific writer who has had bipolar disorder for over fifty years. She is also a Registered Nurse. After writing over 4,000 answers on the popular question and answer website Quora – 800 on bipolar alone – she realized her knowledge, compiled and condensed into books, could really help people.

Sally published her first book, "How to Live with Bipolar" at 73 and has gone on to publish three more books on bipolar. Helping people and their families and friends through the stress and strain of bipolar has become her mission.

Sally is from London and now lives in Texas. She has traveled all over America in an RV and visited many European countries. When she is not writing, she can be found creating stunning oil paintings, doing colored pencil drawings, reading, completing jigsaw puzzles and spending time with Greta, her beloved cat.

Sally hopes her writing will fill in the gaps left by other bipolar disorder books to help people live more fulfilling lives.

I would be very grateful if you would leave a review on Amazon. Reviews are valuable to an author. They help other people decide whether or not they would like to read the book.

Thank so much.

If you would like to discuss your illness you may contact me at:

Website: **https://sallyalter.com**
Facebook author page: **https://www.facebook.com/SallyAlterWriter/**
Email address: **mandala913@omniglobal.net**

www.ingramcontent.com/pod-product-compliance
Lightning Source LLC
Chambersburg PA
CBHW061621130726
47996CB00003B/1077